ACKNOWLEDGMENT!

NO MAN IS AN ISLAND, AS THE OLD SAW GOES, AND WITHOUT THE FOLLOWING PEOPLE I WOULD DEFINITELY BE IN A WORLD OF SHIT....
THANK YOU'S TO:
KEVIN PLAMONDON
TOM BUNCH
ROBERT WEISS
RON TURNER
PETER DAVIS
LONG GONE JOHN
TOM HAZELMEYER
CREIGHTON BURKE
FRED SEIBERT...(TURN TO PAGE 93 FOR THE COMPLETE LIST...)
THIS BOOK IS DEDICATED TO:
RAMONA, WHO WAS WORTH WAITING FOR...

AND LEST WE ALL FORGET WHAT IT'S REALLY ABOUT: EVERY BAND WHO HAS HONORED ME BY ALLOWING ME TO DO A POSTER.

MAN'S RUIN -THE POSTERS & ART OF FRANK KOZIK
©1995 FRANK KOZIK ISBN 0-86719-397-2 1ST PRINTING FEB. 1995
97 98 99 / 5 4 3 2
PUBLISHED BY LAST GASP, P.O.BOX 410067 S.F., CA 94141-0067

2

MAN'S RUIN

POSTERS BY FRANK KOZIK

CONTENTS:

3

Frank Kozik: A Preface by Carlo McCormick

If the medium is the message, then the medium, when twisted in the hands of Frank Kozik, is a message of manipulation, subversion and social critique. An appropriator of trash consumer culture iconography with a ferocious appetite for all manner of visual ephemera that borders on pathological kleptomania, Kozik confronts the vulgar underbelly of the American dream machine by turning its polluting devices back upon themselves, fighting fire with wild-fire in an incendiary purging of the market's hidden agenda. An avid archivist of paper goods, particularly advertising-based propaganda, Frank's work wrestles with the images collectively retained since childhood, the ingrained mundane that you don't think about but still carry around with you as vestigial traces from obsolete programming. Culled from the subconscious like grave-stone impressions of the scars left by the indeterminable onslaught of retinal atrocities we've endured, colored by one of the sickest imaginations and blackest humors in contemporary graphics, what we can barely remember, Kozik simply won't let us forget.

Post-Modernist in mediative practice, Pop in pure aesthetic appreciation, Punk in sensibility, Kozik is ultimately Situationist in his radical de-construction of the spectacle. "Everybody's living in an abstract fantasy world set up by consumerism's need to sell product," Frank explains, "It's all a big sham, and people don't even realize that they are being manipulated". Flexible and fluent in his ability to flip through an extensive inventory of styles, sources, graphic devices and representational genres. Frank's primary concern seems to be less about the media imagery that he chews up and spits out than our peculiar relation to it. A form of lowbrow semiotic discourse carried out on the most brutal level of lowest common denominator intimidation, seduction and hard-sell bullying, Kozik's art of less than subtle persuasion lays bare the way in which people see and process visual information. Or, as Frank puts it; "it's all a big mind fuck."

Bold and aggressive in the strict design concepts he applies to his posters, with lay-outs and color schemes fitting the hard edge paranoia and perversion of his mutant iconography, Kozik's art is the perfect visual vehicle for the generation of bands whose musical excesses, media-damaged sensibilities and cultural disaffections his work has come to represent. "The imagery is on the same vibe-level as the music," Kozik admits, though his independent way of delivering their message is diametrically opposed to anything so literal as band pix, or any such other obvious promotion techniques. Simulating the intensity of the rock scene he has long been affiliated with, his art acts as a pictorial introduction to the musical experience. Keeping it cool and interesting, Kozik,s not afraid of letting it be pretty if it has to, so long as legibility and impact rules. Rife with ironic contrasts, funny and nasty beyond belief, recklessly inverting the super-cute and comforting into creepy, horrific, serious and powerful, Kozik is the mad confectioner lacing his visual candy just to make people think. Perhaps it's because he's not American, but foreign-born (originally from Spain) and now working in San Francisco, via a prolific and ground-breaking period of creativity in Austin, Texas, that he can take the familiar and make it so threatening. Kozik is obsessed with obsessions, a fatal attraction that keeps us buying and keeps the devil selling his seductions. It's an aesthetic of exploitation. "I'm not an artist," he maintains, "this is not an act of beauty or imagination, but of manipulation." Kozik may be quick to point out that "you've been staring at this shit for twenty-five years." Well sure, Frank, but nobody ever made us smell it before.

Carlo McCormick is a noted lecturer and art critic; as well as a frequent contributer to

Artforum, High Times, and Paper Magazine

Frank Kozik : An introduction by Paul Grushkin

Looking at all those nasty rabbits and fucked-up Hanna-Barbera cartoons makes me think that Frank Kozik is one sick puppy. *I'll grant you his poster art is strong stuff.* Is he mad? *Mad isn't exactly it. Profane is closer. Wicked, even.* His art makes him out to be one hotheaded son of a bitch. *His brain is boiling. And he may be out to get even.* With whom? *Unclear. A lot of things seem to amuse him.* He's taking aim at some pretty sacred cows. *Well, he's way out ahead of everybody and you know he's laughing.* He must be an interesting guy, Kozik. *It's almost like his name's become a definition: KOZIK. Crazy shit! Crazy art!* So he's a seriously crazy cat? *He has a screwed-up vision, and his art expresses it.* He's into the underside of American culture. He must give it a lot of thought. *If asked, he'll talk your ear off. But you don't have to buy into it. I do know he just really likes doing posters. It's what he does all day long.* He's making a lot of people nervous. *It's an odd dynamic: Kozik works at being antisocial, but he also likes being noticed. In a strange way his art is very refreshing.* His posters do stand out from everybody else's. *There's no mistaking a warped sense of humor and great cartoon art.* He must enjoy sticking it in peoples faces. *Kozik's an equal opportunity offender. He's loud and he's proud.* Does he know he's pissing people off and blowing minds at the same time? *He'd be the first to tell you.*

In the words of the magazine <u>Your Flesh</u> (interview by Peter Davis and Long Gone John), Kozik, when you ask him for answers, "comes across as an individual with very little tolerance for bullshit. You get ten cent answers to two cent questions (from someone who is both) world weary and wary. He seems to have reached the point where he can't help but see the world around him with the sensibility of an absurdist dramatist. But Kozik says things that provide plenty of good reasons to listen."

Frank Kozik is not the first poster artist—or the first rock poster artist—to be completely "in your face" with his work, or thoughtful and articulate about his art and his world. But Kozik does have the unique experience of finding himself the key personality at an artistic intersection in time and space. Having arrived there, an expatriate Spaniard with Art Maggot roots and no fool he, Kozik strode boldly across, not looking both ways, and gave rock music of the '90s—as well as eons of poster art—a visual taste of a new wackyland.

And what will you find in this brave new world? A veritable treasure trove. Signed and numbered editions of less than 1,000 pieces (some less than 500 pieces) involving intricate 10-color silkscreen process...for next to nothing on the dollar. Kozik wants it that way. Oversize posters-name your poison, he's got 'em. Unusual narrow telephone pole posters-take your pick. And, not to mention some of the most bizarre juxtapositioning in recent memory: Lee Harvey Oswald singing and dying simultaneously! Fred Flintstone shooting up! Amputee kids! Two-headed puppies! Stalin announcing the Melvins!

Just look at it! Is this the work of an modest man? No, absolutely not. Frank Kozik, well spoken as he may be, is not a modest man. Rather, his persona is a beguiling mixture of the cultivated and the crude. His style and substance could only give rise to pulp fiction—did I say art?—played out first, in the grand rock & roll tradition, on telephone poles, then contemplated at full focal length in posh galleries. Like a vitriolic novelist, Kozik's art first stews, then spews. But he's also a highly accomplished silkscreener, and so his finished pieces are more prideful, more arrogant, more <u>finished</u> than those of his contemporaries, like Coop, Kuhn, Pushead, and Pettibone.

"These new artists," attested that good Republican magazine <u>Newsweek,</u> "provide visuals for rock currently consumed by anger and irreverance. So the posters are more anabolic steroid than LSD." Clearly there is more emphasis on color in the Kozik-led rock posters of the '90s than there was in the sullen black & white xerox-driven handbills of the '70s new wavers and '80s punks. But it's not the psychedelic color of the '60s either, despite the neon hues. This is confrontation, not contemplation. A better, though oblique, reference is to the boxing-style art of the '50s and early '60s, with its utter lack of artifice.

Rock poster art—and Kozik has done most of his work in connection with the promotion of rock music events—has evolved to a curious place in the art world of the last thirty years. Rock posters started as throwaway, transitory, and ephemeral creations in the black roots cum Elvis Circus era of the mid '50s. Ten years later, the San Francisco-style psychedelic posters—the Fillmore and Avalon series by Wilson, Moscoso, Mouse, Irons, Kelley, Singer and Tuten, and famous one-offs and mini-series by Griffin, Grimshaw, and Van Hamersveld—shed entirely new, rich, luminous light on poster-making aspirations. Rock art's commercial potential became evident in the '70s with the mega promotion of mainstream and heavy metal rock. Then punk reawakened rock's true anti-establishment sensibility at the dawn of the '80s, and trash ruled. So the swing had to be back to a higher order. And there was Frank Kozik, ready to let loose at 100 posters a year.

Kozik's fans—and they are legion—think of him, in the words of Chrissie Hynde, "in the gutter, but looking at the stars." A hero, but really an anti-hero, a huge talent but also a regular guy, "a craftsman, but not a fucking **artist**," in Kozik's own words. "The one thing I always admired about the punk scene, "says Kozik, "is that it wasn't composed of **artists**. It was more like people doing the extra shit—making stickers and weird little handbills and goofy stupid things so you could have this little piece of something to take home and treasure even though it was just some shitty xerox. That art was such a cool thing, and now I can do it too. But I can make it really good, not to show off, but so somebody can have a totally cool thing like I had once."

The tension in today's rock poster world is between the desire to create the ultimate throw-away cheap thrill—the coolest piece ever which was tossed off but, ha ha, got the biggest laugh— and to create pieces that, like any proud art, might live forever. So where does Kozik get his inspiration for this dashed-off, yet immediately classic stuff? The lamest TV cartoons, the most obscure British war books, Ed Roth-style hot rod caricatures, '40s girlie mags, tabloids snatched off of washroom floors. And yet the resulting art is immaculately silkscreened, a true craftsman's achievement and a collector's bonanza, all making for a fine contradiction that everyone around him admires.

"I hope people don't take it all too seriously," Kozik opines. "I hope they can take it for what it is. Posters are just drawings. Even big silkscreened posters. They're just things, not the world. You know, the Big Boys used to have this saying on their records: 'Thanks for buying, now go out and start your own band.' That's the way I think it should be: do your own drawings, say your own piece. You know, perform a good deed—piss somebody off."

Paul Grushkin is the author of THE ART OF ROCK : POSTERS FROM PRESLEY TO PUNK (Abbeville Press, NY 1987 and 1993).
He is a managing partner in Company X Apparel LTD.

6

OBLIGATORY RANT:
BEING THE MERCURIAL RAVINGS OF THE CONSUMMATE PISS ARTIST -OR- HOW TO DROP OUT OF HIGH SCHOOL AND MAKE A MILLION DOLLARS.

THAT'S RIGHT, PAL, HIGH SCHOOL DROP-OUT. HOW WELL I REMEMBER THE SNEERS OF THE TEACHERS AND MY FATHER'S FURY. BUT HEY, HERE I AM AT THE TOP O' THE HEAP (WELL, HEAPLET, AT LEAST), THUMBING MY NOSE WITH IMPUNITY AT THE TEEMING HORDE LABORING AT THE FOOT OF MY OWN, PERSONAL, IVORY SUMMIT. LOOKS EASY, DON'T IT, WELL GUESS WHAT- IT IS. EVERY DAY I AM ASKED, "GOLLY,,, HOW DID YOU DO IT? WHERE DO YOU GET YOUR IDEAS?" SORRY TO SAY, I DON'T KNOW, AND BY THE WAY, NO IDEAS ARE INVOLVED. ALL I DO IS CONSUME THE MOUNTAIN OF PAP THAT SURROUNDS US AND EXTRUDE IT IN WHAT I THINK IS A MORE PALATABLE FORM, NOT UNLIKE A BLUEBERRY FLAVORED MUFFIN LOAF FOOD PRODUCT. AS FAR AS ANY TALENT OR "ARTISTIC" ABILITY IT SIMPLY BOILS DOWN TO SHEER GOOD LUCK AND RECOGNIZING A GOOD BREAK WHEN I GOT IT. ALL THE REST IS MERELY EXPLOITATION AND PERSEVERANCE. IT'S SIMPLE, REALLY, I HAVE JUST GIVEN WAY TO THE INNER IDIOT IN ALL OF US, WHICH I MUST SAY IS AN AMUSING STATE TO BE IN.

FRANK KOZIK
SAN FRANCISCO, JANUARY 1995.

★PS: THROUGHOUT THIS BOOK YOU WILL FIND A RUNNING COMMENTARY ON THE POSTERS AND SITUATIONS WHICH SURROUNDED THEM. I HAVE TRIED TO BE CONCISE AND ALL THE WHILE CLEVER, AND IF A FEW OMISSIONS OR ERRORS OCCUR, WELL, I'M ONLY HUMAN AND IT'LL GIVE YOU A CHANCE TO PUT YOUR OWN TWO CENTS WORTH IN...

The Real Deal

Allright, now that I've got the 'assholism' taken care of, I will try and lay out a little history of all of this and talk about the numerous people without whose help nothing would ever have happened.

I always liked to draw as a child - the usual stuff boys draw - battleships, castles, explosions - no savant level stuff, so no one ever took real notice, all I wanted to be was a scientist... or maybe an astronaut. Well, bad grades and glasses took care of that. In 1976, I came to the US and promptly began to fuck up in general, dropping out of school, getting high, joining the service. Military life took me to Austin, Texas, where I ran into Punk Rock. I started to go to as many shows as possible, and before long fell in with a group of fellows, (the Artmaggots), who where doing your basic mail-art street xerox thing. So I hung out, went to shows, left the military and got high a lot, for years actually, drifting through a million blue-collar jobs all the while. Then I got lucky. I met Brad First.

Brad had operated a series of music venues in Austin, and in 1987 he opened the doors of the Cave Club. I got a job there as a doorman, and before long started doing posters. Brad was the first club owner I had ever run across that valued posters, and not only was he willing to pay for them, but he actually wanted them large format and in two colors! I was in heaven, and cranked out as many as he would let me. Response from the street and the bands was enthusiastic, and before long doing local posters became a steady thing. Through the auspices of recognition in the Austin Chronicle, I was able to parley it all into a job doing graphics for a large-size T-shirt shop. There I recieved a more or less instant hands-on education in the mechanics of printing, separations, and line-art production. After a year spent doing less than "cool" designs I took my new found technical knowledge and hit the streets, freelance. It was while sharing space with several better-known Austin artists that I had my second stroke of luck. In through the door walked Robert Weiss. Weiss was instrumental in opening up new areas of work for me, and a brief foray into the "Fine Art" world culminated with my first show at the Luz de Jesus Gallery in Los Angeles. During this time I cobbled together the makings of a silkscreen shop, and with the help of Tom Bauman, a true rennaisance man if there ever was one, I began to produce the large format concert posters. Well, life being that way, my relationship with the people in Los Angeles soon soured, and I pretty much figured it was over, but hey, third time lucky. I met Kevin Plamandon. He and I have worked together closely and are today on the verge of the next big push, (you'll have to wait until the next book), but most of what has happened in the last three years is basically, well, his fault.

Being an "Artist," (personally I prefer the term "Graphic Designer," or poster guy, or whatever), and being successful at it is not an activity performed in a vacuum, it is a collaboration involving a lot of hard work by a lot of people. Let me tell you about some of them.

Back in Texas, Tommy Bauman helped to not only actually build the shed the first print shop was in, but showed me how to typeset on a computer, mix colors, and about a thousand other things. Once the press got rolling I had to find a good printer. Enter Lindsey Kuhn, a hell of a good printer whose perseverance, attention to quality, ingenuity, and willingness to work some long hours made about 100 posters possible. The undisputed master of Wackyland between 1991-1993, his iron hand held sway over other Wacky crewmembers Chad Helms, Shane Valentine and Lee Roy Chapman. Today Lindsey is a highly respected poster artist in his own right and the owner of Swamp Industries. I must also make mention of Kathy Hill and Richard Whiteaker, owners of Graphic Arts, whose generosity and fine filmwork will never be equaled.

After moving to San Francisco, Wackyland-Pacific soon kicked into action under the direction of Ann Stauder.

The current crew consists of Shop Manager Tony Short, head printers John Van Hoose and Grady Broyles assisted by Jason Voisone and Joel Moeschl.

How the poster deal works - It's easy, I am contacted by a band, venue, booking agent, label, or promoter. They want a poster. I print up about 700 of them. Out of this run 100-150 are sent to the show site to be used for promotion. This is free. To pay for it all, I secure permission to sell a numbered edition (usually 500, sometimes less), this pretty much pays for the printing and puts a little money in my pocket. Everyone benefits and no one has to spend any money except for a fan that wants a poster. It's a simple concept,and it works.

Physically, all posters are silkscreened on 110 lb index stock. We use an American Cameo 38 single stroke automatic. All inks and chemistry are TW Graphics waterbased 5000 series, air-dried. I cut all the separations by hand and they are burned onto 220 count yellow mesh on hand-stretched screens using a 5KV single-point light source. Dig it.

Last but not least, how this book was put together. First off, thanks to Ron Turner whose interest, financial generosity and never ending patience (this suckers a whole year late!) made this book possible. It was layed out on a Mac Power PC 8100/80 by the Mighty Nick Rubenstein of Bunker Suicide Graphics using all kinds a shit I can't even think about.

REMEMBER, KIDS...

"SNOOZERS ARE LOSERS!"

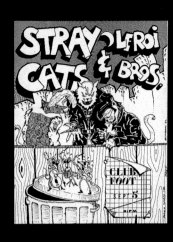

CRUDE BEGINNINGS 1982

GODFATHER OF SOUL

THIS ONE CHANGED
UNIVERSITY OF TEXAS
BOOKING POLICY

AN AMAZING SHOW,
MAYBE 20 PEOPLE
SHOWED UP

THE BUTTHOLE
SURFERS' DISCO BAND

SEVERAL PIANOS
WERE DESTROYED

SNOTTY GUYS REALLY
PROUD OF LONG HAIR

FURTHER MAYHEM

FROM SUCH HUMBLE
BEGINNINGS

1982 – 1990: HUNDREDS OF 1 OR 2 COLOR POSTERS WERE DONE FOR SEVERAL AUSTIN
TEXAS CLUBS – 6 OR 7 A WEEK, ALL DONE AT NIGHT OR DURING LUNCH.

VERY RARE POSTER - MAYBE
100 WERE PRINTED - REY
WASHAM SUPPLIED THE PAPER.

NOT FOR SALE EXCELLENT
DICKS SPINOFF BAND

THE VERY FIRST TWO-COLOR
POSTER

THE GREAT SEEDBED OF A
BAND PLAYS AGAIN

THE CAVE CLUB IN AUSTIN FEATURED A GREAT SPECTRUM OF THE BEST LOCAL AND
TOURING ACTS. SCRATCH ACID MEMBERS DAVID YOW & DAVE SIMS WENT ON TO
FORM RAPEMAN AND THE JESUS LIZARD.

OFFSET POSTERS

THIS ONE DROVE THE ULTRA-PC
DALLAS PAPERS WILD

THE LEGENDARY SONIC YOUTH
PLAYED WITH TOTAL COMMITMEN
TO MAYBE 200 PEOPLE

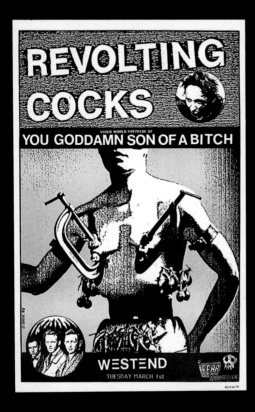

THE FAKIR SHOWS HIS FLAIR
FOR FASHION

LOTS OF SMOKE AND PROPS ON
THIS SHOW BUT THEY DID ROCK

12 POSTERS ARE STARTING TO HAPPEN FOR TOURING ACTS AND OUT OF TOWN GIG
THE SEED STARTS TO SPREAD.

THE EMBRYONIC BLUES
EXPLOSION

MAINSTAYS OF THE
AUSTIN "ART SCHOOL"
SCENE

LATE 80'S NOISE

HELMED BY TIM KERR

DISCO

SON OF DISCO

BEYOND THE SON OF
DISCO

DISCO 2: THE WHITE
MAN'S BURDEN

EVEN YET STILL MORE
DISCO - HEY, IT PAID

SLOW WEEKS WOULD BE LEAVENED WITH POSTERS FOR LOCAL "DISCO NIGHTS" –
WHILE NOT TOO MUSICALLY SOUND, IT ALLOWED FOR SOME INTERESTING GRAPHICS.

OFFSET POSTERS

WHY LIMIT CHRIST TO THIS PLANET?

I'VE STILL GOT THE
SINGLE

THE PEP BOYS

PHOTO BY ANTVEIL

THIS EVENT NEVER
HAPPENED... OOPS!

14

TWO COLOR POSTERS ARE NOW BECOMING THE NORM.   AT THIS POINT I AM STI[L]
GOING OUT AND PUTTING THEM UP

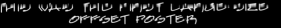

THIS WAS THE FIRST LARGE-SIZE
OFFSET POSTER

(SHOWS 11 MINUTES) I BREAKS
– ART

THIS DESIGN LIVED ON FOR
YEARS ON T-SHIRTS, ETC.

THE HAIR FETISH ANNOUNCES
ITSELF

LATE 80's TEXAS WAS THE BEST PLACE TO SEE THE BUTTHOLE SURFERS AT THEIR
CREATIVE PEAK – SOME OF THE BEST SHOWS I'VE EVER BEEN TO.

OFFSET POSTERS

I FOUND THIS LITTLE DARLING WHILE ON LSD... PHOTO BY ANTWEIL

FIRM & FULLY PACKED

ONE OF THE RAREST— ALL BUT TWENTY WERE DESTROYED WHEN THE CLUB WENT BELLY UP BEFORE THEY COULD PAY THE PRINTER!

HIS LAST SHOW PRIOR TO CARDIAC ARREST

DISCO INFERNO

MY CHARLES BURNS RIP-OFF

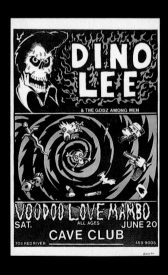

SKULLVIS

OH... SHARON....

16

THE XEROX AESTHETIC — YOU'VE GOT 5 DOLLARS AND AN HOUR... BUT, HEY, IT WORKED.

OMINOUS THUNDER

COMMON LAW CABIN

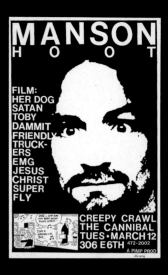

THE VIBE WAS THERE

METAL AS SHIT

THIS ONE BROKE THE CAMELS BACK

TRIPPY, DUDE

FLUIDS DID SPEW

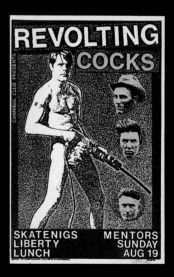

"HERBIE"

OUR LADY OF THE FLACCID
PENE

VENUS OBESA

LA PRIMATIVA

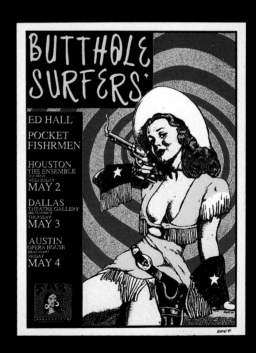

ROUND 'EM UP COWPOKES!

 18 I STEP UP TO FAKE 4—COLOR PROCESS — THESE ARE ACTUALLY 3—COLOR PRINTS, WHICH TAKE A WEEK OF HAND—CUTTING ZIPATONE APIECE TO DO...

THE PRINTERS SCREWED THIS ONE UP, BUT IT LOOKED COOL THAT WAY.

RANDY DUPONE. PHOTO BY ANTVEIL.

SEE BELOW

MASQUE OF THE RED DEATH

THE MONKEY AND STRIPPER WORE MATCHING COSTUMES. THE BONUS WAS THAT THE MONKEY WAS TRAINED TO REMOVE THE EXOTIC'S CLOTHING TO THE BIG BEAT... HISTORICAL FACT!!!

OFFSET POSTERS

SOUL POWER

BLISS BLOOD'S HAPPY
CREW

THE BEST BAND IN THE
WHOLE WIDE WORLD

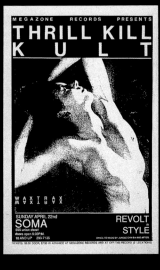

ANDROGYNY EXPRESS

HOO-HOO FOR
COCOA PUFFS

PHOTO BY LISA
BRENNAN

HOO-HOO FOR KHALI

ECSTATIC FISHBOY

ATTICA - 1971

20   A TASTY SAMPLER OF BLACK AND WHITE GEMS...

THINK ABOUT IT...

PHOTO BY ANTWEIL

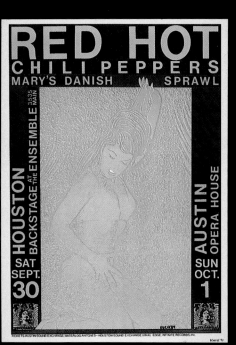

OFFSET POSTERS

ELECTRONICALLY
AMPLIFIED MUSIC

THE FIRST AND ONLY
FILLMORE POSTER... EVER.
GO AHEAD — SUE ME.

TOO SHORT RULED... EAZY WAS A LIL' BIT TIPSY

POP-EYE, DALLAS, TX!

I AM A CURIOUS BLUE...

THE NWA SHOW WAS INSANE — 10,000 PEOPLE IN A RODEO SHED IN TEXAS...

HOT DOG!

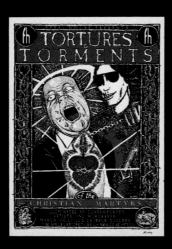

THE THREE STIGMATA
OF RICHARD RAMIREZ

TOOLIN' FER YER
INTESTINES...

CRACK— THE BREAKFAST OF
CHAMPIONS

STEPHANIE'S PISSED / PHOTO BY
ANTVEIL

BLAND DESIGNER JOB

THE KILLER 3-HOUR
GROOVE

TORTURES AND TORMENTS WAS THE   BEGINNING OF A FINE ASSOCIATION WITH
FERAL HOUSE WHICH CONTINUES TO THIS DAY...

FOG MACHINES, LIGHTS, & A RAT
IN A JAR

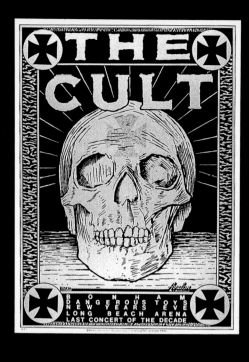

NICE HAT, BUDDY

MMM... GOOD EATIN'

HEY, YOU WERE INTO IT...

 24 BORN ON JAN 9, 1913, A POOR SHARECROPPER'S SON... RICHARD M. NIXON WAS TO
ONE DAY ASCEND TO THE PINNACLE OF SUCCESS IN AMERICA...

DIE ÜBERSHIKSA IST TODT

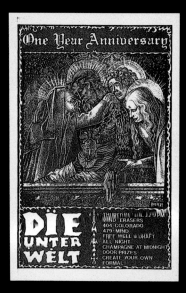

RECIPE FOR FAILURE

RECIPE FOR SUCCESS

HEROIN — LUNCH OF CHAMPIONS

HITTIN' IT BIG IN THE FATHERLAND*

*THIS HUGE FORMAT BAD RELIGION POSTER WAS MY FIRST 4—COLOR JOB... NOT KNOWING WHAT THE FUCK I WAS DOING, IT TOOK WEEKS...

THE FIRST SILKSCREEN
POSTER

TURNABOUT IS FAIR PLAY

THE FIRST SILKSCREEN
POSTER

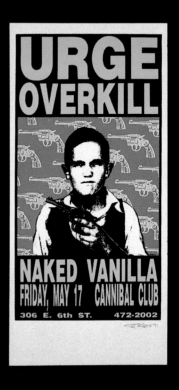

THIS PHOTO WAS
FOUND AT A TEXAS
GARAGE SALE

26

AFTER YEARS OF PAINFUL HASSLES WITH PRINTERS, THE DECISION IS MADE TO DO
OUR OWN PRINTING VIA SILKSCREENING. EDITIONS WERE VERY SMALL.

YERNUSIAN JAZZ COMBO

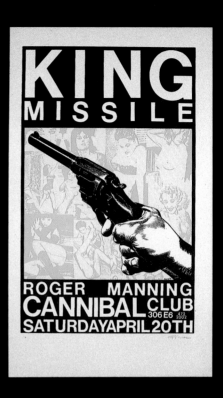

THE RIGHT TO ARM BEARS

SILKSCREENS

THE FIRST
APPEARANCE
OF THE DEVIL
BITCH

PAPIST DRONE

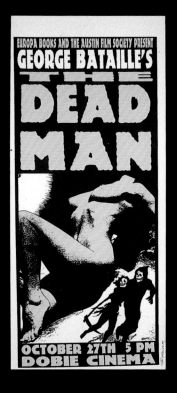

GOOD BOOK, LOUSY
MOVIE

MR. HAPPY TOOTH

PRECISION
ENGINEERING

THE FACE OF
EVIL*

*ADAM PARFREY WAS STUNNING IN THIS SPOKEN WORD APPEARANCE, CHICKEN SUIT
AND ALL...

TO LEE HARVEY, WITH LOVE

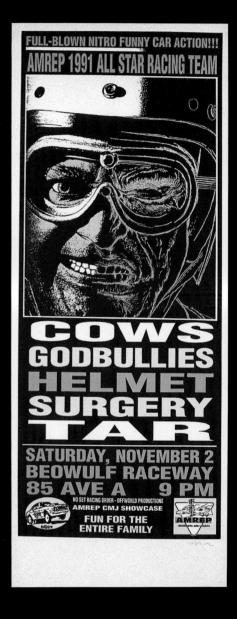

SNOOZERS ARE LOSERS

FIRST BITS O' FLUFF FROM AMPHETAMINE REPTILE RECORDS RECORDING ARTISTS.
THE INDEPENDENT LABEL.

29

SILKSCREENS

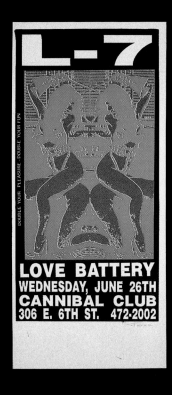

DOUBLE YOUR
PLEASURE

BONER PONY

SPEED'S MYSTERIOUS
OLDER BROTHER

EAT MORE BEEF

LUCK WOLF
(20X30) MIXED MEDIA ON BOARD

PORK SAUSAGES AIN'T KOSHER
(20X30) MIXED MEDIA ON BOARD

THE RED ANGEL
(20x30) MIXED MEDIA ON BOARD

**WRESTLEMANIA 1941: JOE "MAN OF STEEL" STALIN
VS ADOLPH "THE HITMAN" HITLER**
(20x30) MIXED MEDIA ON BOARD

33

34 MARY JANE ROTTENCROTCH AND HER PEARLY PINK PANTIES
(20X30) MIXED MEDIA ON BOARD

MISS FORTUNE
(20X30) MIXED MEDIA ON BOARD

TRIBUTE TO PRESTON BLAIR
(20X30) MIXED MEDIA ON BOARD

DRAGSTRIP PSYCHO
(30X40) MIXED MEDIA ON BOARD

MR. LUCKY'S FRESH STEP
(20X30) MIXED MEDIA ON BOARD

38

30 DAY KAHLI DIET PLAN
(20X30) MIXED MEDIA ON BOARD

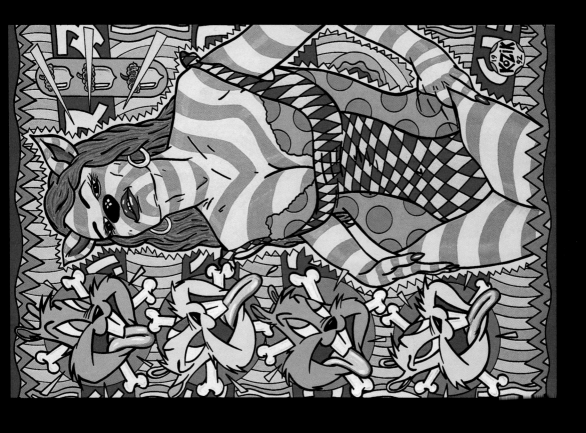

FROM TINY ACORNS DO MIGHTY OAKS GROW
(20x30) MIXED MEDIA ON BOARD

POWER TO THE PEOPLE
(20x30) MIXED MEDIA ON BOARD

ROUSING INSECT TALES
(20x30) MIXED MEDIA ON BOARD

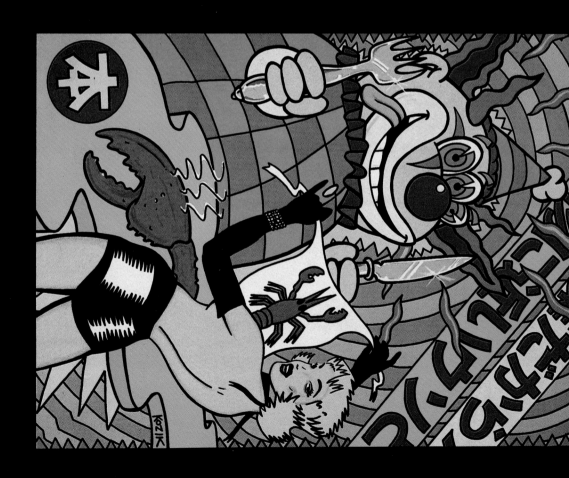

SURF AND TURF
(20x30) MIXED MEDIA ON BOARD

40

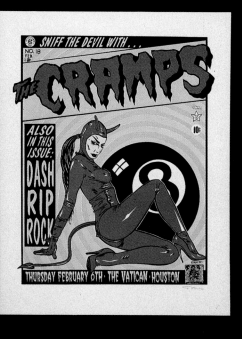

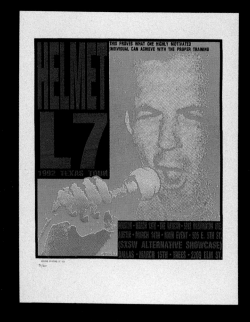

G.B.Y.J.P.*

EXPRESS YOURSELF

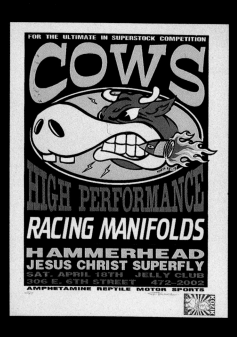

MUCHA RIP-OFF

FULLY BLOWN BOVINE FURY

*THIS CRAMPS POSTER INAUGURATED THE "NUMBERING SYSTEM."
IT BEGINS WITH 92-001...

41

SILKSCREENS

PUMPIN' ON
BETA CAROTENE

THE FIRST
APPEARANCE
OF THE
PROTO-SARCOPTY

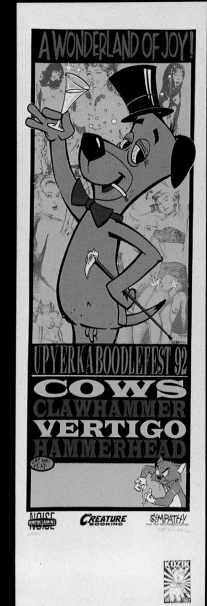

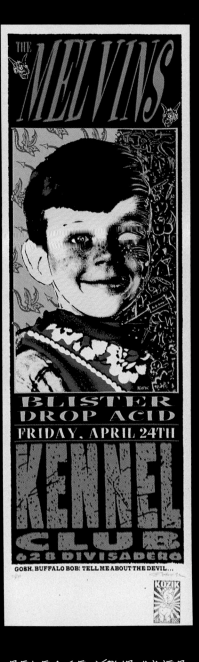

RELEASE YOUR INNER CHILD

BEELZEBUB

SOUTHERN FRIED SPOCK

SHADES OF VENCES

TO SUFFER CUPIDS
SLING

HADUKORU-PANKU-RAKU DES

 AS A YOUNG MAN, RICHARD NIXON GAINED A NAME FOR HIMSELF BY THROWING A SILVER DOLLAR ACROSS THE MIGHTY LOS ANGELES RIVER.

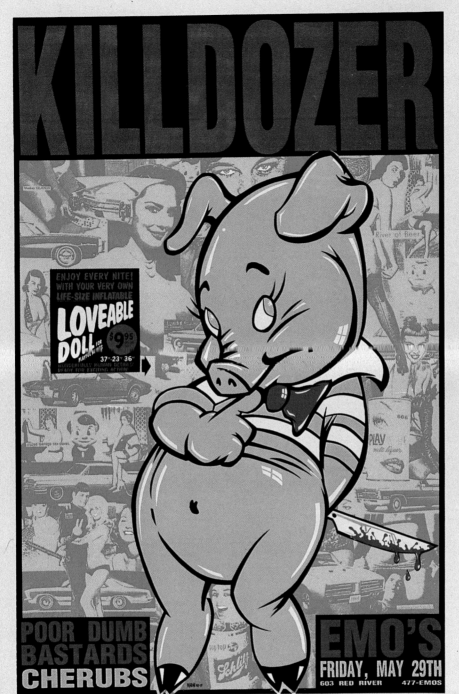

THE UBIQUITOUS WEE WIDDLE PIGGUMS IN HIS DEBUT SILKSCREEN APPEARANCE.
HE SHALL RETURN...

45

WINTER

SPRING

SUMMER

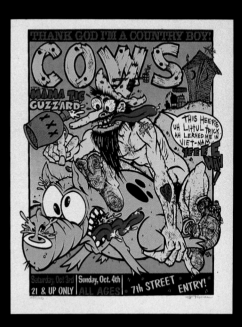

FALL

CELEBRATING THE FOUR SEASONS... WITH ALL CREATURES, GREAT AND SMALL.

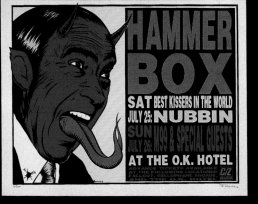

THE FATHER OF LIES

SUCH... POSTURE

SILKSCREENS

A HOT TIME IN THE OLD
TOWN TONIGHT

"THESE ARE YOUR
CHILDREN"

MR. CROWLEY'S DEATH
MASK

x

   THE 11.5" X 35" WAS DESIGNED FOR USING ON TELEPHONE POLES.

NATCHEZ BOUND*

IT'S THE SAME OLD STORY

ROLLER BOOGIE EXPRESS

*NATCHEZ WAS THE PARTY TOWN IN THE MID 19TH CENTURY. A COMPLEX OF SALOONS, "THEATRES" AND BAWDY HOUSES THAT EXTENDED FOR MILES ALONG THE FACE OF THE NATCHEZ BLUFFS.

VITAMIN H

EVERYBODY NEEDS A DADDY
LIKE CHARLIE

 I HAVE OFTEN PONDERED THE FATE OF MR. MANSON'S OFFSPRING.

THE LITTLE COMMIE THAT
COULD

7 COME 11*

SILKSCREENS

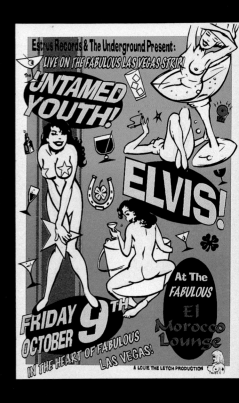

LIL' SARCOPTY BURSTS
UPON THE WORLD

"NUFF SAID"

SIAMESE BIMBOS

PIGGUMS II

MASS MURDERERS — THE GUNSLINGING HEROS OF OUR TIMES.

BLEEDAGE!

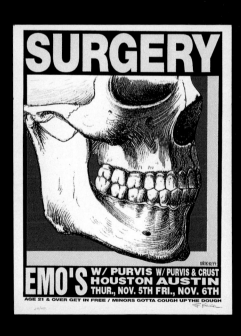

THE LEGENDARY EMO'S*

A TRIBUTE TO GLOBE

THE FATHER

THE SON

THE HOLY GHOST

1992'S BUMPER CROP OF FINE ART PRINTS.

JIMI

YOUR FLESH

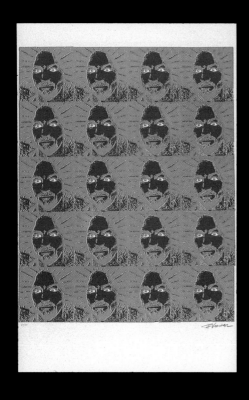

EVERYTHING'S CHARLIE

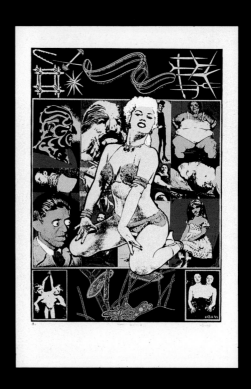

FRENETIC GENETICS

MISS FORTUNE

MR. JAMES OSTERBERG

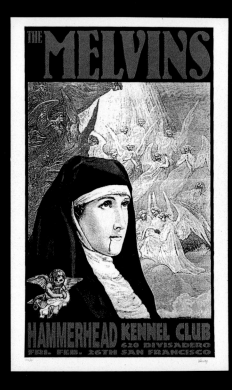

BRIDE O' CHRIST

'EASTER EGGS FOR TOJO

WACO APOCALYPSE MEMORIAL

OUTDOOR SPORT*   LA VERONICA*

 58

*THESE TWO WERE COMMISSIONED BY RECORD RUNNER IN MADRID — THE BEST
ALTERNATIVE MUSIC STORE IN SPAIN... MAYBE THE ONLY.

MISS 1977

THORAZINE STATION

SILKSCREENS

WE NEVER SLEEP

SHANTY IRISH... AND PROUD OF IT.

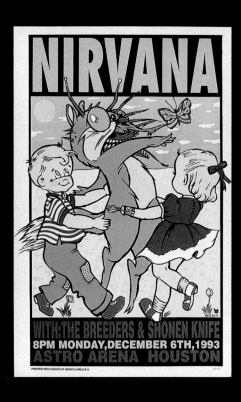

HOPE IT'S A BETTER PLACE

SORRY DAVE...

60 1956: KOREAN WAR HERO RICHARD M. NIXON SETS A NEW ACE RECORD BY DOWNING 6 MIG FIGHTERS IN ONE DAY, EARNING HIM THE CONGRESSIONAL MEDAL OF HONOR.

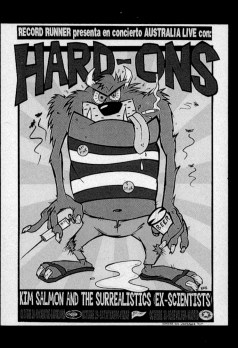

AUSTRALIAN PUNKS IN SPAIN?

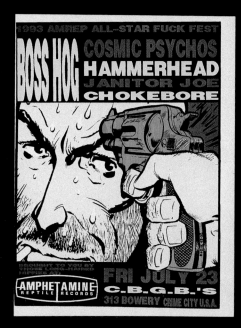

UNREST. . . STILL, U.S.A.

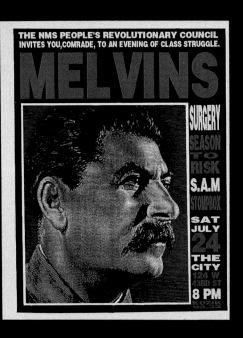

UNCLE JOE

REPUBLIC OF MANCHUKO

AMERIKA ÜBER ALLES

OUR GREAT NEIGHBOR
TO THE NORTH

MURDER CITY

I START TO GET TO FUCK WITH OTHER COUNTRIES... COOL.

NIGHT OF THE HUNTER

HUNTING WABBITS

BUMMER!

A NEW SUN RISES IN THE EAST*

WHEN LIFE WAS SIMPLER

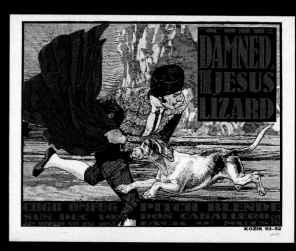

WOT'S IT MEAN? —PROF. R.J. GUMBY

  *I FINALLY LAND A GIG FOR JAPAN, THIS BRINGS ME NO END OF PLEASURE.

CHRISTINA, QUEEN OF THE JUNGLE.

THE GREEN MUSE

TROPIC DREAMS

CAP'N AMERICA & BUCKY

66 1958: AFTER A WHIRLWIND TOUR OF AMERICAN CITIES AND NUMEROUS TICKERTAPE PARADES, RICHARD NIXON PARLEYS HIS WAR RECORD INTO A SUCCESSFUL BID AS MAYOR OF PHILADELPHIA.

SKID ROW

EXPOSURE OF THE CONVICT
STAIN

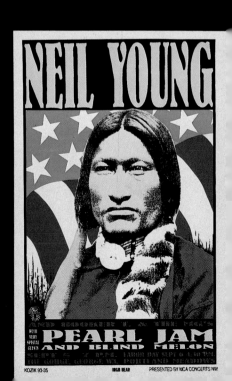

DAZED and CONFUSED

WORLD PREMIERE
The Paramount Theatre
September 16th-8:00 pm

after show party at ACROPOLIS-(70's fashion encouraged)
BENEFIT FOR THE AUSTIN FILM SOCIETY **$10**
Sponsored by:The Austin Chronicle and KGSR 107 fm

POLIO LAD

KEROKEROKEKHALI

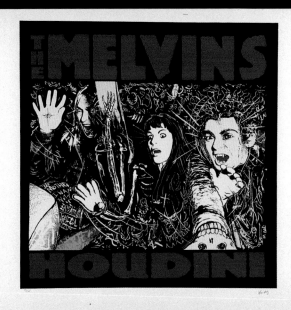

TROUBLE DOWN UNDER

HEY, ART...

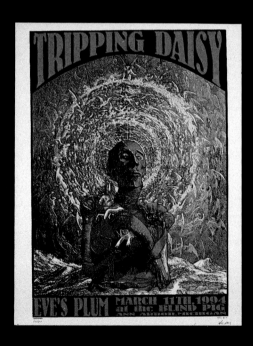

HEY, MAX ERNST...

HIGH STAKES

THESE ARE THE LAST 4 POSTERS PRINTED IN TEXAS BY THE STEADFAST ORIGINAL WACKYLAND CREW.

SAFETY FIRST!

GREEN DAY

WITH SPECIAL GUEST:

TILT

TUESDAY, APRIL 5TH

THE OZ

SEATTLE

Produced by MCA Conerts NW
KOZIK 94-6   PRINTED AT WACKYLAND PACIFIC

The Exotic South Seas Stylings of

the Useless

Playboys

Trailblazers

Thursday July 28th

The Bottom of the Hill

1233 17th St. San Francisco

KOZIK 94-14   printed at Wackyland Pacific

TITS   &   ASS

MR. SHORTS' DOPPELGANGER

NICE... PROSTHETICS...

FLIPPER WAS MY VERY FIRST PUNK
SHOW, AEONS AGO...

AN INSANELY GOOD BAND

ONCE IN SAN FRANCISCO, I START THE POSTER TRAIN AGAIN.

CRAWL, WORM

A VERY MERRY CREW

1968: RICHARD NIXON TURNS DOWN HIS FORTH TERM FOR MAYOR OF PHILADELPHIA IN HIS BID FOR THE PRESIDENCY. AMERICA'S FIRST POPULIST BLACK PRESIDENTIAL CANDIDATE RUNS UNDER THE MANDATE, "POWER TO THE PEOPLE." POLLS PREDICT A LANDSLIDE VICTORY

A COY LITTLE FELLOW

LIQUOR IN THE FRONT, POKER IN THE REAR

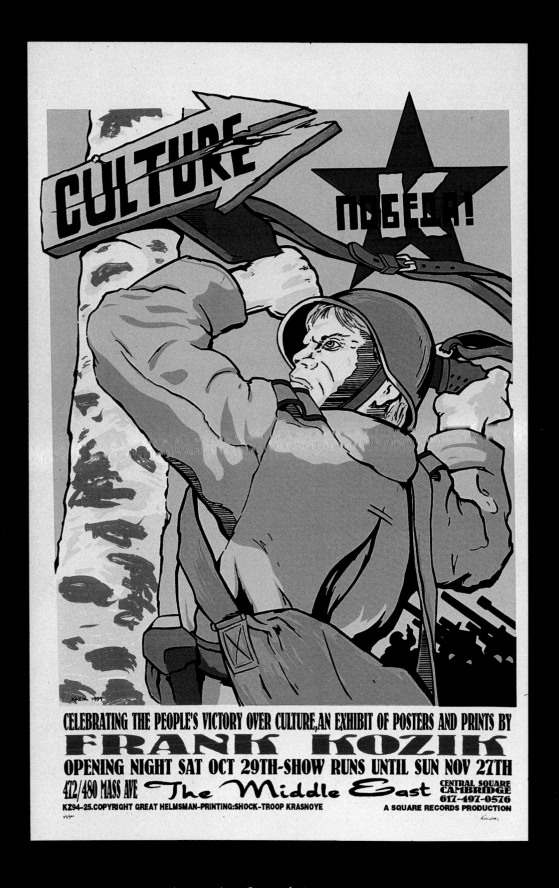

HOMAGE TO MY FOREBEARS

1968: ON THE EVE OF VICTORY, NIXON'S TRIUMPHANT MARCH TO OFFICE IS DESTROYED BY ALLEGATIONS OF MORAL TURPITUDE. DETAILS ARE VAGUE, THEN NIXON SHOCKS THE NATION WITH A PUBLIC ANNOUNCEMENT THAT HE IS GOING TO "TUNE IN, TURN ON, AND DROP OUT." FAMOUS NUDE APPEARANCE AT LINCOLN MEMORIAL 2 DAYS LATER.

79

TWEEDLE DEE   TWEEDLE DUM

I'M SORRY, YOGI...

SWISS MISS

WITH MEASURED TREAD

BOB MOSES, MOVE OVER

THA OLD TIME RELIGION

PANIC IN NEEDLE PARK

NINE INCH NAILS

MARILYN MANSON
JIM ROSE CIRCUS SIDESHOW
SEPT. 1994 24TH SEATTLE CENTER ARENA

KOZIK 94-26

SNEAKYVILLE PRINTING

ALL IS ONE

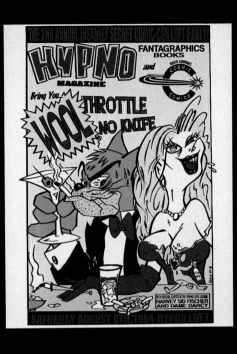

TOM'S GONE HOLLYWOOD

POR LA PATRIA

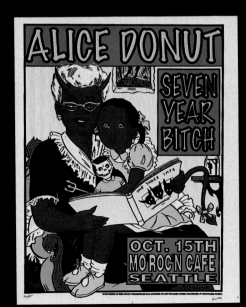

VICTORY OF THE PROLETARIAT

BY 1974, WITH THE WAR OVER AND THE YOUTH MOVEMENT IN DECLINE, NIXON DROPS
FROM THE PUBLIC EYE AND BEGINS A 10-YEAR DOWNWARD SPIRAL INTO DRUG AND
ALCOHOL ABUSE, CULMINATING IN HIS FORCIBLE INSTITUTIONALIZATION.

85

...LET'S KILL SOMETHING!

A COZY PAIR*

 86   *I ACQUIRE COMPUTERS AND BEGIN SOME NEW FUN...

ORIGINAL SKIN

 1984: CLEAN AND SOBER, AT LAST, NIXON DECLARES HE IS "BORN AGAIN IN CHRIST," AND HE OPENS THE TOWER OF POWER AND LOVE MINISTRY IN GULF SPRINGS, MISSIPPI.

KILLDOZER

SAT NOV 19TH with MOUNT SHASTA and MOUSE TRAP O'CAYS CORRAL
504 E. WILSON
MADISON WISCONSIN

PRINTED AT WACKYLAND PACIFIC

PHOTO BY ANTWEIL

1990: IRS AUDIT FORCES NIXON'S MINISTRY TO CLOSE SHOP. UNDER A WAVE OF PUBLIC SCORN HE RETREATS INTO THE HALLS OF HIS SHERMAN OAKS RETREAT.

GOD DIDN'T MAKE LITTLE GREEN APPLES

995: IN A FINAL, PATHETIC BID FOR PUBLIC RECOGNITION, NIXON SURFACES BRIEFLY IN A TV SITCOM PILOT ENTITLED "DICK'S WAY" AS THE CRUSTY YET LOVEABLE BUTLER "DICK." THIS COMEBACK ATTEMPT WAS CUT SHORT BY HIS DEMISE AT AGE 82, AFTER COMPLICATIONS FOLLOWING KIDNEY-STONE SURGERY. RICHARD M. NIXON, THE PENULTIMATE 20TH CENTURY AMERICAN HERO.

PIC

DISKS

SEVEN INCH COVERS

The Now Sound...

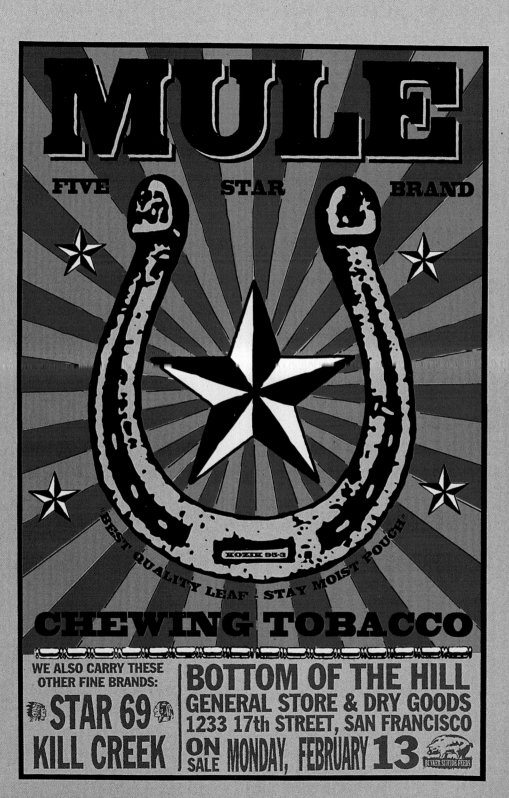

MORE PEOPLE I OWE... Abby Antweil, Al Smith, Tony Short, Ann Stauder, Brett Gurewitz, Jay Blakesberg, Pat Blashill, Bliss Blood, David Lienhardt, Scott Bowlin, Loren Barnard, Lisa Brennan, Blake Simpson, The Beastie Boys, Black Market Flowers, Gibby, Paul, King and Jeff of the Butthole Surfers, Jim Blanchard, Glenn Bray, Andrew Bennet, Blag, Jack Boulware, Mike La Vella, Spike, Cabaret Magazine, Preston Blair, Liz Penta, Joe Coleman, Chris Cooper, John Hawkins, Tommy Steele, CZ Records, Chad Hensley, Johnny Craig, Larry Cartmell, CSG Ammunition Sales, John Cantwell, Mark Dancey, Tim Moss, David Warner, George DiCaprio, Don Donahue, Dave Cryder, Lurker Grand and Idil Vice, Greg Escalante, Emo's Crew, Eric, Dave, Kumbala, Spanky, Jason, Feral House, Russell and the Fuck Emos, Walter Schultz, Paul Grushkin, Kathy Hill and Richard Whiteaker at Graphic Arts, Mike Gerald, Micheal Goldberg, Dale Grover and Buzzo, Don Blackstone and Gashuffer, Gordon Clark, Jim and Debbie Goad, Rex at Hypno, Ed Hardy, Igor Mortis, Micheal Howard, Julie Proschekova, John Kehoe, Jay and Harry Knowles, George Kucewicz, Krystine Kryttre, Deborah Valentine, John Lambert, Lynne Keller, Ivan Lerner, Lydia Russell, David Livingstone, Lydia Lunch, The Ladish Bros., Michelle Longhurst, Mike Laird, Martin Stricker, Billy and Alix at La Luz, Todd Kasten, Darren Mock, Carlo McCormick, Robert and Stella Morehead, David Lufkovitz, Tim Cronin, Mike Morasky and Steel Pole Bathtub, Michelle Vitetta, MCA Concerts NW, Paul Mavrides, Larry Kay, The Middle East, CBGB's, Otto at NiceMan, Miriam Linna, Jim Gibson at Noiseville, Jelly Helms, Niko, Patrick Rogers, Danny O'Connor, Barbar O'Dair, Deb Pastor, Julia McHugh, The Hawaiian Prince, Scott Griswold, Jim Straitedge, Tim Kerr, Richard Mather, Tommy B, Micheal Priest, Danny Garrett, Lindsey Kuhn, Shane Valentine, Lee Roy Chapman, Jennifer Conrad, The Mighty Doktor Pizz, Adam Parfrey, Lynne Porterfield, Jacabor Kastor, Racheal from Pervis, Jerome Crooks, John Valania, Norman Thecat, John Pound, Jan Quirk, The Red Aunts, Los Tios de Record Runner, Rocket from the Crypt, Pat Dillon and Tammy Kizer, Rina Neiman, Mark Rubin and the Bad Livers, Jake Wiseley, David Yow and the Jesus Lizard, Savage Pencil, Sonic Boom, David Sandlin, Patrick and Roger at Sound Exchange, Subpop, Winston Smith, Sean (RIP) and the Surgery Crew, Jon Spencer and Christina Martinez, Gwar, Steve McConnell, John Cladwell, Caprice Carmona, Liz Gazzano, Charlie Todd, Max Fox, Dave and Tree, Billy Pittman and the Useless Playboys, David Levine, Robert and Suzanne Williams, Uncle Charley, Howard Schomer, Dave Minert, Jason Fiber, Jon Winston, John Kelly, Jennifer Smith, The Happy Hour Bowling League, Rich Malley, Spot, Biscuit, Fred Gretz, and all the great landlords who let me slide on the rent over the years....

List of Fancy - Schmancy Gallery Shows:
Solo Shows:
1992 La Luz De Jesus Gallery, Los Angeles, California
1992 Artrock Gallery, San Francisco, California
1992 CBGB'S 313 Gallery, New York City
1993 La Luz De Jesus Gallery, Los Angeles, California
1993 CBGB'S 313 Gallery, New York City
1993 Chicago Cartoon Gallery, Chicago, Illinois
1994 The Weathered Wall, Seattle, Washington
1994 The Tap Gallery, Sydney, Australia
1994 CBGB'S 313 Gallery, New York City
1994 Zurich, Switzerland
1994 The Middle East, Boston, Massachussettes
1995 The Metro, Chicago, Illinois
1995 America Obsessed, Spirit Square Center for the Arts, Charlotte, North Carolina
1995 The Razor's Edge, Providence, Rhode Island

Group Shows:
1991 Bess Cutler Gallery, Santa Monica, California
1992 Psych-Out Group Show, San Francisco, California
1992 Graphix 1 Show, Bess Cutler Gallery, New York City
1992-on The Jimi Hendrix Exhibition - Traveling World Exhibit
1993 Pop-Komm, Koln, Germany
1995 America Obsessed, Spirit Square center for the Arts, Charlotte, North Carolina

Permanent Archive:
Barker History Center, University of Texas, Austin
Cooper-Hewitt Museum, New York City

Well, there really isn't one, because the damn
thing runs to about 15 pages. We have a fairly
complete list, and if you reeeeeaaaaally need it,
send five bucks to the address below.
Man's Ruin
610 22nd st #302
SFCA 94107/Poster List

Also...a second volume of posters and art covering
1994 through 1997 will be available through
Last Gasp in December of 1997.

Thanks for reading the book!
-Frank Kozik
San Francisco, 1997

MAN'S RUIN INC.

PURVEYORS OF FINE ART POSTERS, AND MUSICAL RECORDINGS.

MAN'S RUIN
610 22ND ST #302
SAN FRANCISCO
CA 94107
SEND $1 FOR CATALOG

"QUALITY OUT THE ASS"